THE PAIN...

THE PROCESS...

THE PROMISE...

JENNIFER JOHNSON COOK

ISBN NO. 978-1-943409-81-5

Printed in the United States of America

Pure Thoughts Publishing, LLC

www.PureThoughtsPublishing.com

Table of Contents

Greetings:

Hello, I absolutely appreciate you for making this choice! Thank you for allowing me to enter your space to chat for a while. I totally enjoy using what life has taught me to teach others. I can assure you that this will not be your typical book. This book reads more like a conversation between you and me. In no way am I saying that things will happen for you the exact same way they did for me. We were all created different. I am asking that you have an opened heart and mind while reading this book. I also ask that you take in what is meant for you. I do not believe that this book has been written for no purpose. It is for the betterment and assistance of your growth! You are going somewhere; you are doing greater things in the earth and this book is designed to assist you on your way. Maybe not your "Finishing Touch" but most definitely a needed additive in this recipe of LIFE! It is to you that I say" THANKS!" If you are not already doing so, please follow me via

Facebook @ The Birthing Chamber Unlocked

Or

Email: BirthingIt18@Gmail.com

Introduction

When God is taking us to a place called "PROMISE" we must understand that it will not take place without a process. Regardless of how long or intense the process is, you must know in your heart that in an appointed time and place, it will happen. Much like birthing, you will experience the pains associated with the process. I am here to discuss some of those details to show you the similarities of the two. It was not until a few years ago that I saw this likeness for myself. I do not always have the same experience while on my way to PROMISE but, part of that is because most of the time the destination is different. Each journey to promise has its own painful process. A seed for instance, after the ground has been prepared for it to be planted it is then set in a hole, watered and covered up. This seed is no longer in the light that it was in. Now it is in a dark place alone. You must be okay with the aloneness of the journey or you will forfeit the journey for a walk in the park! Just because both are moving does not mean they are both going somewhere!" It later sheds off the outer layer that we saw prior to planting. It then releases what was placed on its inside. None of this takes place before it dies to its will that is may become what THE FATHER has destined it to be. You cannot go to PROMISE with your own will, it must be the will of The Father. Therefore, we are not to despise the dark places that we sometimes find ourselves in. It is in those dark places that we can be real and expose ourselves to the process in complete surrender. This is the only way we will grow. So, after this step it begins to come into its purpose, it was only meant to be a seed until it was planted. Apparently, the seed is aware of this because after a while we see proof on top of the ground that purpose is being re-leased. Nobody goes back inside of that hole it was planted in with a reminder to get up! After you accept your purpose the same is so. Fast forward, the seed, though only one may have been planted yields a plenteous harvest. You are not here to do just one thing! God placed inside of you the ability to do MANY things, however, just like the seed you must be planted in good ground, loose yourself of the way the world knows you and surrender to PURPOSE, the way The Father designed you!

It is okay to LET GO during the PROCESS..........

May 2003 my husband and I were two of the most excited people on planet earth! This was because we closed on our second home! I still remember the joy that filled both of our hearts, we were OVERJOYED! Being able to move to the city limits where we were able to take bike rides downtown with the kids and take strolls to the park, it would be so much fun! We had a goal, we wanted to be in a home by the time we were married five years. We worked fervently towards that goal and we accomplished it. We were so grateful that though the Vision tarried we waited for it and it was unfolding well. We both had good pay-ing jobs so there were no worries as far as the finances were concerned. We had our Pastor to come and pray over our home and declare

Blessings over our family. We moved in and invited everyone over to celebrate! Proud was an understatement. The feeling of AC-COMPLISHMENT consumed us. We had so many family gatherings in that home! Then there was 2004 when I got pregnant with our son. That was another big Blessing, we wanted a boy so, we went to the doctor and found out that was exactly what we were having! We felt much like the sun was shining on us! New house, New baby, New life......
Sounds ideal huh? Well, it was up until I had to go out of work while pregnant. We did not see this coming none whatsoever. Three months into this pregnancy I began having sciatic nerve pain. The pain began being so great until I had to see a doctor about it. My doctor referred me out to a specialist. Sometimes a regular doctor cannot properly diagnose us, in those cases a specialist is necessary (the same is so in life.) I went to the

specialist and he recommended that I rest at first. Later, in this book you will see the details of that. I ended up having to go out of work. I was no longer able to work at only four months pregnant; do not forget we had just bought a home. So, now all those bills that my husband and I were splitting equally were now all his responsibility. I felt horrible about the fact that I was unable to help him financially. I was supposed to be able to help him! It was then that I tried to get SNAP benefits, only to find out my husband made too much money and I did not want to lie on my application. Thanks be to God we literally fell perfectly in the Medicaid guidelines. I felt a little better that at least we were getting some help with the medical bills. I still remember feeling somewhat helpless as my body grew more and more weak as the baby got heavier. Rodney assured me on several occasions that no matter what we would be just fine. He always maintained such big faith. So, I did as much within the home as I possibly could. Cook, clean, make sure he had lunch for work, help our daughter with homework. Just anything to free him up from having to do anything once he got off from work. He still spent quality time with our girls on his time off and did an excellent job listening attentively to all I had to say about everything. Well, me being able to clean and cook did not last long at all. My body was growing weaker trying to tolerate the irritated sciatic nerve. I eventually got bigger in the pregnancy and he got more and more comfortable on that nerve. After my belly grew to a certain point the doctor stopped me from driving. This was HORRIBLE news to me. Who was going to take our daughter to school and pick her up? How will I get to the grocery store to buy the things that we needed? How will I get to my doctor's appointments? These were just a few of the questions lingering in my mind. Thankfully, our village came through for us in big ways! They literally split up the various duties and the cooking also. All I had to do at this point was BE PREGNANT! Cool, right? No! Not as cool as you think. Though the help was second to none I felt so bad to know others were stopping their plans to help take care of me. There I was crying my eyes out because we had help and I felt bad. I was not crying because I was prideful, this was because I was independent and now life caused me to be totally dependent upon the help of others. Along the journey to PROM-ISE you are going to need the help of others that you can depend on and that is totally okay! Well, they totally ignored me and continued to HELP!!! I remember having to use the mobile cart in the stores because I was not able to walk long distances. I remember the looks on the faces of the people when I came rolling through in that cart at only 27 years old. I guess I looked too young to be in a mobile cart. I honestly had to do it because I was not capable of walking on my own for a long period of time. AFTER ALL, our son did spend five months on my sciatic nerve. So, there we were with a new style of living after just buying a home and having two daughters that were both under six years of age. Well the details of that delivery are further down but, let us just say after I had him and came home, we were a family of five with no food stamps and more mouths to feed "AND THE LORD SAW US THROUGH!" As you can imagine the bills got somewhat out of hand going from two paychecks to one. Just when we thought the storm was passing over, we found out that our taxes were escrowed based on the senior citizens that lived in the home prior to us. So, not only were we behind in our mortgage we were BEHIND IN OUR ESCROW ACCOUNT! How could this be? We went over the paperwork, we asked a few questions at the closing, we did our price shopping! Somehow, we missed that! So, now we are behind in a payment that is having to go up and it is now September of 2006 and we have no savings. I thought I was just calling the mortgage company to plead for some sort of payment arrangement for the arrears. There I was finding out that our payment will now be almost double of what we were paying and to find out our mortgage rate was not fixed but adjustable! We felt a sense of anger beyond one's wildest imagination. We felt cheated and taken advantage of. So now, we are being EVICTED! Both of us had jobs at this point yet we had sunk everything we had in the home making repairs and trying to stay afloat. It made us feel even worse that we were not losing the home in a time where only one of us were working. At this point both of us were working and this happened! Embarrassed was an understatement for what we were. We did not want anyone to know what was happening to us so we hid it, we had to move in a single wide mobile home that was less than half the size of what we had gotten accustomed to living in. We had to explain to our kids that we were moving and that was easy until we showed them where we were going. I know that as a man Rodney's pride was shot. This did not mean that he was not a great provider for his family we were just misinformed and went into a deal without full knowledge. We were young and did not know all the right questions to ask. If you are in the market for a home, know all these things beforehand. That was a valuable lesson. So here we were leading the line just before a lot of others went into foreclosure in 2006. We were so embarrassed to say the least. We did not even tell our sweet neighbors that we were moving. We moved 11:00 at night so nobody would know. That is just how ashamed we were. We were ashamed that we trusted people at their word instead of doing our own homework. We were ashamed that we trusted people that were in trustworthy positions and took complete advantage of an opportunity. Most of all, we were ashamed to simply LET GO! What would people think of us being that we are both working, and this awful thing has happened. How will we explain this DOWNGRADE to our kids? How will we recover from the funds that we sunk into this home before coming to the realization that it is simply time to let go? These were some of the questions that we had during the journey to promise. Yes, I do believe that even this was a part of the journey!

As a human race we often dislike change. Most of us prefer everything to remain the same. We will suffer greatly just to keep everything the way it has always been. Many of us take drastic measures just to be able to keep it the same. Unfortunately, this is not always the right thing to do. Change, though it does not always feel good it is in fact working for our good whenever we are in Christ. Being moved from one's original placement is never easy for it is in this place that we found comfort, though we may have forfeited peace! Bear in mind that in order to get to this place in life that we are currently in, we had to be moved from the womb, THAT WAS COMFORTABLE ALSO! Change is then found inevitable- ACCEPT IT! The world is changing as we breathe!

We could have saved so much money if we just would have LET GO when it was time. I do not blame us because we only did what any person would do, fight to hold on. We did not realize that this was the beginning of a process that was going to take us to the promise. We did not know it was okay to LET GO!

A butterfly for instance is not birthed in its final state, it must undergo a PROCESS that releases its PURPOSE. In the beginning stages a butterfly is just an egg, until it becomes a caterpillar that in no way resembles its full PURPOSE. Whenever I see a butterfly my mind does not even think about an egg nor a caterpillar. This is because the butterfly is so pretty until it takes away from my mind whatever it once was. The Beauty that God desires to release through you is going to cause others to forget your process. However, this in no way exempts you from this process. You still must go through. Pain helps us to appreciate the process to purpose. That thing that hurt you the most yet pushed you to purpose, you will NEVER forget. It is when we arrive at PURPOSE that somehow the pain does not sting as bad then it eventually dissipates.

Process is defined this way by Meriam Webster: a natural phenomenon marked by gradual changes that lead toward a particular result

If you want to see something different take place you must be open for change. A small change can happen in a matter of seconds.

whereas the bigger changes take place over time.

Process takes time. We must be okay with the time that PROCESS takes. It is imperative that we understand fully that GOOD things come to those who WAIT!!! We must wait if we want things done right. It is not always good to have a microwave mentality. Some things happen quickly while others take time.

The Pain, The Process, The Promise

_____

_____

_____

_____

_____

_____

_____

_____

_____

_____

_____

_____

_____

_____

_____

_____

_____

_____

_____

_____

_____

_____

_____

_____

_____

_____

_____

It got better when I realized I was NOT being PUNISHED!

We saw what was happening to us as punishment at that time! Now it was time to move and resettle. Over half of my household decorations had to be placed in storage because we did not have the room to bring all the stuff that we had from the BIGGER house. Imagine going from a 2072 square feet home to less than half that size. I was so hurt and ashamed. I still remember hiding my car so nobody would know where we lived. When people asked where we lived, I would tell them the general area, but I would not be specific. I was ashamed. Not of where we were living but of how we got there. Never be ashamed of a process God allowed you to be a part of! I could not explain then how we made it with no problem with only one job and soon as I went back to work, everything went haywire. Could it be that less really is more? How is it that this thing is happening NOW? I was angry with God for a little while. Wondering why He was punishing us as faithful as we were. We worked in the church, we paid our tithes, we gave of our time and talent in the community. Why was this thing happening to us? Surely God was upset with us. Surely, we were being punished. That is at least how I felt. Rodney's concern was basically the same only for him it was worse because he is the man of the house! I cried more during that time that I ever did. If we learned anything it was "Everything happens for a reason and this was not a punishment!" We also learned how to be grateful in whatever situation we discovered ourselves in. Many will believe that when things of this magnitude happen surely, you must have done something wrong, or being punished for past sins. It was in that small home that I came to grips with the exact truth that God sometimes shifts us not because He is angry but because He desires our attention for the information He is planning to impart. No, I am not trying to say we did everything right and it was no fault of our own that this thing took place. I am saying that God's MIGHTY hand was at work the entire time. We were in no way being punished. He took us through to bring us out therefore I see that He was with us the ENTIRE time. Let me say this, the entire time we kept going to church, we kept paying our tithes and we kept sharing our time and talent with the community. We were hurting inside, and we had a few unanswered questions at that time, yet we kept sharing the GOOD-NESS of Jesus to everyone that we saw. You will get through the process a lot smoother if you find an opportunity to serve. We poured into people from a pure place. When people contacted us about the blessing of receiving their new home, we celebrated with them. My husband and I never allowed what was taking place to infiltrate the love and compassion that we both have for mankind. I am so grateful that we kept a good attitude about our time of testing. That does not mean it was not hard and we did not hurt we just realized it was a part of God's plan and we were not being punished! Do not become bitter about what feels like punishment. Take Joy in knowing everything happens for a reason. You will find that the energy you put into a thing is the energy that will be reciprocated. You are not being punished!

The Pain, The Process, The Promise

_____

_____

_____

_____

_____

_____

_____

_____

_____

_____

_____

_____

_____

_____

_____

_____

_____

_____

_____

_____

_____

_____

_____

_____

_____

_____

_____

_____

ACCEPT IT!

I will say that nothing changed for us until we began to accept what God allowed. I think my husband accepted it quicker than I did. I just could not believe how this thing was unfolding. I think my pride was also a hindering force in accepting it. I have learned that to be found eligible for advancement to the next level we must accept and conquer every part of the level that we are on now. God makes no mistakes. When we are in Him, we can ACCEPT THE PROCESS for what it is. A process only makes you better if you submit to it. The hard part is denying our own will and agenda and accepting the will of God. See, we know what we want, we just do not have a clue what He wants for us, well at least not in detail. I honestly thought that we would live in that house forever. That was my plan, that was also my husband's plan. However, it was not God's plan. Denial is a weed that can choke off a beautiful plant. We must pluck that thing out before it destroys the entire garden. This is not the only thing in life I have ever had to accept that was against my own plans but, it was a big one. Accept what God has allowed to take place. God sometimes uses what we thought would work to work an even better plan out. Truth is if we try to change it, we will only make a mess out of it. Give it to God and let Him be GOD! At the end of the day all we really ought to desire is HIS WILL, HIS WAY! God is aware of where you are. We tend to only think of it this way when everything is working according to the way in which we want it to. We think God is only in the "Good" of what happens to or for us. I am here to tell you that sometimes, He signs off on the stuff that we consider to be the devil! Consider Job. There is nothing that satan could do to Job apart from God's permission. When we are in Christ, we can ACCEPT the change. Not just accept it but know in our hearts that IF He leads us to it, He will in fact lead us through it with the same grace! As a child it was always so hard for me to accept the answer of NO! That word would ring in my ear hours after it was spoken. I hated being told NO. As I grew, I taught myself to always meet people's expectations of me and this would cause them to say yes rather than no. I later learned that the only reason that they were saying yes was because I was following their idea for my life. This is a miserable life to live! Do not ever allow others to dictate your life to avoid accepting the truth. A hard no is better than a misleading yes. Folk will be with you if you go along with their plan for your life. You do not want this. Many go along to get along so that they can avoid having to seek God for themselves, or to avoid the ridicule of having their own opinion. As a result, they depend on others to tell them what to do, where to go and who to be with. That my friend is a PUP-PET! The reason why there is not a space provided for a hand to fit in your back is because you were not designed to be a puppet. Accept what is, it may hurt, you may even have to cry but ACCEPT IT! As a child I did not like taking castor oil so I would spit it out. My mother consistently gave it to me because she understood I would get over the taste if I just accepted it. She knew the desired results that she had in mind; I was just unaware. Sometimes the quicker we accept the things of life the quicker we can get better. Do not fight what you ought to accept, it only makes your process longer. I am not telling you what I heard but, what I know…… I am also not telling you to lay in self pity and gloom after accepting it, you are responsible for getting the assistance necessary after completing your first step of ACCEPTANCE!

_____

_____

_____

_____

_____

_____

_____

_____

_____

_____

_____

_____

_____

_____

_____

_____

_____

_____

_____

_____

_____

_____

_____

_____

_____

_____

_____

PAIN

Pain is defined in the Meriam Webster's Dictionary- **Pain is defined in the Meriam Webster Dictionary this way: the physical feeling caused by disease, injury, or something that hurts the body. : mental or emotional suffering : sadness caused by some emotional or mental problem. informal: someone or something that causes trouble or makes you feel annoyed or angry.**

Pain is not something that we look forward to. It is the idea of it for some that causes pain all by itself. Nobody signs up to be hurt or have pain inflicted upon them in any way. I know for me it is a NO! However, PAIN is often the sign that something is taking place. When an expectant mom goes into labor PAIN is usually what she feels. The pain may start mildly, it could also be so faint some do not even recognize it is there. For them it is just an ordinary uneasiness but nothing major. Nothing to sit down and cry about. In fact, some women keep working as usual while experiencing the pains that are associated with Labor. For others, not so much. Everyone has different levels of pain tolerances. Some can take a lot of pain others cannot take anything. For me in my last physical pregnancy that pain began early. I experienced labor pains a few weeks before giving birth to our son. The pain was so great for me that my doctor prescribed pain medication for me to take specifically for this pain. I often tried to go without this medication, but it was not possible. A lot of other mothers told me at that time that it was not necessary for them to take medication for pain during their pregnancy. It made me feel as though something was going wrong with my pregnancy. I felt this way because I was comparing my pregnancy to those around me. That my friend was the wrong choice.

I have learned that two people can experience the exact same pain yet be affected differently. That is perfectly normal. While I was pregnant with my son, I used to hurt so bad that some days I was literally in tears. Yes, the pain was just that great! The further along I got the more I hurt. We have three kids and I did not hurt this way with the other two. My son rested on my sciatic nerve while inside of me. For those that are unaware, the sciatic nerve is the longest nerve in your body. It starts in your lower back and splits to run through your hips, buttocks, legs, and feet on both sides (WebMd.com). There were times that I would have to lift my leg using the pants leg of my garment it was just that numb. My OB/Gyn sent me to the chiropractor however, it was here that I was informed that having an adjustment done could possibly cause early labor and I could have lost our son. I was not having that. It was from this that I learned sometimes while in painful situations any adjustments made could possibly make your bad situation worse. Yes, it would have felt better to be free from it all but my idea of free could have caused me to lose the promise. So, to you I say you may not be physically pregnant with an actual baby but even during your Spiritual pregnancy sometimes it will get painful. There will be times when it feels like an adjusting in the plans could make things so much better. You must realize the fact that this could also make things worse. Hang in there the darkest hour is just before light. I simply trusted God, went out of work and endured the painful PROCESS because I wanted THE PROMISE! When your eyes are fixated on THE PROMISE, nothing stands in your way. NOTHING!

Oftentimes we give up on the way to THE PROMISE because we somehow lose our focus. You must consistently remember your WHY! Why are you on this road? Why did you say yes when the Lord assigned this to you? Things like this help us to remain focused and keeps us from giving up. I slept in a recliner for five months. It was very, very painful but it was even more painful to get up out of the bed, so I simply stayed in the chair. While on your way to THE PROMISE you will find that your ("Regularly Scheduled Program") maybe altered at times. You may not have the opportunity to enjoy the pleasures of life as you are accustomed to. It is called sacrifice. To whom much is given, much is required. You may have to be inconvenienced for a while; this all goes back to remembering your WHY! I originally bought the chair that I had to sleep in for my husband a few months prior. Boy was I glad I made that purchase! I had no earthly idea that I would need it so soon. He was so Sweet in adjusting to the SHIFT that I was in. You will need folk with you that can roll with the punches. While headed to THE PROMISE sometimes the shifts that affect you will also cause those around you to be affected. If they are not in it to WIN, you will find out at the point of SHIFTING. You will not have to decipher as to who is with you or not with you, just keep going you will see. Ever had a bug on your vehicle till you get on the road and begin to ride? What happens to it when you begin to ride off? It falls off right? It simply fell off because it was never supposed to be there, your windshield was just a comfortable spot for the time being. That is why when the winds began to blow, it could not last. You will find this true in your Process! Do not fight this part, simply allow it to take place. You will not need all that extra baggage when you arrive at your PROMISED DESTINA-TION! It simply is what it is, no love lost, no feelings hurt, and life goes on…. But, back to what I was saying………

The pains of life are sometimes just this great! You may have lost a loved one due to death, that is painful. You may have lost your job, that is painful. You may have lost the idea and reality of your dreams, that is painful, you may have lost a fake friend, THAT IS A BLESSING…. See, what caused you pain may not cause the next person pain however, in no way does that negate the magnitude of your pain in your experience. As I said earlier, we all experience pain differently. The truth about the matter is......those pains may limit your mobility as well. Just like I told you that I lost the feeling in one of my legs during pregnancy with my son. This somewhat im-mobilized me. I had to accept that this was happening and strategize how I was going to keep going. This is another reason why you only want solid people in your corner, the process is not the time to be holding on to fake folk or building relationships with inse-cure ones. You are going to need someone to help hold you up because THE PROCESS is work! I am a firm believer that everything happens for a reason and a purpose. We must get in tune with God to see what the reason for such great pain is. The reasoning for this was to make me stronger. At least this is how I feel. It made me pray more, lean on God more. It made me delegate more and it also made me accept help! As a norm I try to do as much on my own (with God's help of course.) as I possibly can. However, there will be times in life where it will be necessary to assign tasks to others and that is perfectly okay. I learned all of that through pain. What has your pain taught you? When we realize that it did not happen to us instead it happened for us, we will get through it smoother. I talked about this in my other book and it is obviously the principle that I live by. I had to make this conscience decision to be at peace when things happened that I deemed as unfair, unfortunate or uncanny towards me. I even had to use the pain from my pregnancy to work for me. There is a lesson in everything if we take note! It is when we allow the things that cause us pain to make us bitter and distressed that we open a door for even more pain. Your pain is not by happenstance, it has a purpose. It may not be revealed right now but if your mindset is right towards this whole ordeal you will have a better understanding of it. I know this firsthand.

I want you to understand that your pain is not totally for you it is partly to make you better that you may be able to help someone else along the journey to PROMISE! You may feel isolated as it pertains to the most recent pain that you felt. It may feel as though these type things only happen to you. It hurts even greater to know that the world is looking on with their jokes and interpretations as to why this is happening. All of this is NORMAL! I have been there. The laughingstock of the room only to go home and be angry at myself. I had to realize that this too has happened for a reason and bringing me pain was evidently a part. Because I understand the Lord will never put more on me than I can handle, I had to consider deeply that I was made for this! Not to be the joke of the room nor take the pressure that came with the joke. Yes, I have walked away from some crowds feeling smaller than an ant at a picnic, but I had to realize that some people cannot handle such joking. Some people would have broken under this type pressure. I had to know and accept that it was not happening to me, instead it was happening for me.

The way that we give our pain purpose and meaning is to tell what we have overcame. This releases us from it in a sense. When you begin to see how your story will help someone else you will truly be amazed. I am not saying go buy a bullhorn and release your story in the neighborhood! I am saying be sensitive to the timing to share. You may be speaking with someone about what they have experienced that is like what you made it out of, help them with your testimony. Remember when giving advice always give Godly advice. God did not allow you to make it through all that pain and process without allowing you to reach PROMISE and to reach others! You will reap the PROMISE of your suffering if you just hold on and go on through. Romans 8: 18 King James Version says it this way, "For I reckon that the sufferings of this present time are not worthy to be compared with the glory which shall be revealed in us." Whatever it is!

_____

_____

_____

_____

_____

_____

_____

_____

_____

_____

_____

_____

_____

_____

_____

_____

_____

_____

_____

_____

_____

_____

_____

_____

_____

_____

_____

_____

The way out is THROUGH!

A few years back I preached a message entitled "The only way out is THROUGH" within this message I talked on how we desire the blessings of God apart from the PRESSING of God. Well, it does not work that way. In order to receive the PROMISES, you are going to have to endure the PAINFUL PROCESS! Yes, you could always cut the line and advance yourself to the front however, that is the best way to get to the bottom fast. Many have slept their way to the top, cheated, lied, back stabbed, manipulated and kissed up, just to name a few ways of self-promotion. Authentic promotion comes from God. I have learned that quick is not always correct. Many will agree to going through pain if it is in fact quick and painLESS! Understand this, you cannot have pain without feeling the sting of the PAIN! We do not want to suffer, wait, endure and be steadfast. I am not saying that all we should desire to do is suffer hard times. I am saying that when we do endure and suffer those hard times, we will be blessed for doing so. Whatever it is that you find yourself in know that it is working for your good.

The pains of my pregnancy were in no way fun, yes there were times that I wanted to just scream but I held on. See the only way out is THROUGH. Whenever God gives us instructions to follow or even a Promise to work towards, it does not mean that we will go straight to it without any trouble. You are going to have to go through the steps for getting to THE PROMISE! If you are going on a trip and you set the GPS up to guide you there and it gives you the estimated time of your arrival this does in no way negate the fact that you will have to drive. Yes, you may be looking at the final destination on the GPS, but you cannot jump inside of that machine. You will have to drive to get to where you are going. Here is the kicker; the weather may get bad, the car may give you problems, the people inside the car may begin to complain that it is taking too long to get there, but when you heard YOUR instructions CLEAR none of that will matter, In fact it will be of none effect when your eyes are set on THE PROMISED PLACE! That my friend is called, PROCESS! GPS is only going to tell you how to get there and suggest the safest route. You are responsible for the work in getting there.

The Pain, The Process, The Promise

I am in no way an avid exercising person; however, I do fully understand the concept. I understand that the first few days are the absolute worst! I have tried it a time or two and experienced firsthand the burning pain that comes with entering a workout regimen. I have started and stopped more than a few times. Had I completed the beginning stage I probably would have been in better physical shape by now. See the burn is temporary but the results are lasting. The second set of days are better but still painful.

I remember my husband worked out with some friends and his pain was so great that I literally felt sorry for him. There were times that I wanted to take the pain away from him, but he had to endure his own process. That is sometimes where we mess up in the process. We cannot complete the process for those that we love. Whatever God has for us to do we have to do it our own self. Stop trying to detour someone else's process because you feel sorry for them. Whatever God has allowed them to go through they were built to endure it. We can only lengthen their process by trying to intervene. It is perfectly okay to hurt when someone else hurts, but we cannot take on their pain. One day you will have your own process to endure and if you burn yourself out carrying someone else's weight then you will have to deny your process and that is not good.

Notes

_____

_____

_____

_____

_____

_____

_____

_____

_____

_____

_____

_____

_____

_____

CAKE BATTER

If someone is baking a cake after reading their recipe, they still have to put it all into motion. The process will have to be carried out in order to get the desired results. Think about it this way......

It requires many ingredients, much like life. To make cake the proper way one must be certain to include all of the necessary ingredients and the correct amount. After putting in the correct amount of the proper ingredients it must be stirred consistently that they all may blend in together well. While doing this you may notice that the consistency of these ingredients appears rather inconsistent, sloppy and even very pliable. It is at this point that we must remember the finished result that we desire. If we forget what we desire this inconsistent, sloppy bowl of batter to be we will at that moment lose the momentum to continue. Life is the same way at times. It does not yet appear what you shall be. We just have confidence that we have the necessary ingredients to make something GOOD out of THIS! SO, we press, after completing the stirring process we pour this batter into a pan that is the shape of the cake that we so desire. For example, if I want a round cake, I use a round pan. If I want a square shaped cake, I simply use a square shaped pan.

So, after we have decided the shape, we want our cake to be we proceed in pouring this batter into the pan that we want the results from. What you are supposed to be has already been placed inside of you it just takes a process to reveal it. Unfortunately, it is not done at this point. There is yet more work to be done.

Now we must place this batter in an oven that is at the desired degree of heat for the type of cake that we are baking for the suggested amount of time according to the instructions. After staying in the oven for the recommended amount of time we then have to test it to see if it is in fact done. If it is not done, we have to allow it to bake a while longer testing it periodically to ensure its readiness. Even at this point we are still not done. After the cake is done baking and the tests have all been passed now our cakes must be placed on the counter for a specific amount of time that they may cool. Now it is time to be prepared for the icing to be applied. After this process it is then ready to be sliced and served.

This whole process is amazing to me! The fact that the finished work in no way resembles the process in which it had to endure just to be sliced and served. So, it is with us as

Servants of Jesus Christ. You may say nothing about cake batter has to do with you. To you I say, "I firmly disagree!" If you pay close attention to this process you cannot help but see the similarities that they have.

_____

_____

_____

_____

_____

_____

_____

_____

_____

_____

_____

_____

_____

_____

_____

_____

_____

_____

_____

_____

_____

_____

_____

_____

_____

_____

_____

Pain and Process produced A Servant

Consider that you were knitted and woven together as a fine tapestry, that took time. Breath was blown into you which brought you into your being but before that the DNA of your parents came together and shaped you. That is why you resemble them or someone in the family line. See once we say yes to Jesus and mean it from our heart, He then releases what we need to be MADE over! He will not allow us to be served out to others before we obtain the proper ingredients in us properly prepared and finished so that we do not cause infection in THE BODY! All too often folk are rushing this process. These are the most important steps. Do not rush being made OVER! There are people out here that need your authentic original gift. The one that was placed in you long ago. It is when the process is rushed that we run the risk of poisoning a lot of innocent people. Thus, we have broken people helping broken people and the result is anger, frustration and malice. See, we must realize when we are getting the ingredients for the process and stop rejecting this important step. You need those eggs of life that you thought were hate tactics because God is making a cake. You needed that HEAT in your life to process you in order for you to be developed properly. Yes, it may have appeared that everyone else was completing before you, but the fact of the matter Is this, GOD WANTED YOU COMPLETE!!! You could not come out before the rest, you needed to be developed. Some cakes require a longer process with more intense heat. But when you are done, you are then ready to be served to many and then they will have the encouragement to begin their own process. Do not despise the day of small beginnings, you will reap if you faint not! This is a proven fact!

All of what I have told you thus far has formed together and produced a Servant out of me. Sometimes in life it felt as though I was being slighted. It also felt like others did not want to see me prosper at times. Because of the way things worked out in some cases. I was often left feeling as if I was the only one going through at that time and that may have been true. However, I had to accept that it was working together for my good. I witnessed firsthand as my "Cake Batter" stage unfolded. Not as it was taking place but when I took an aerial view of my life. Sometimes we are too close to see what is really going on, back up! Like the eggs in the batter, I had to yield to the process. There is a difference between "Giving Up' and "Yielding"- Giving up means I no longer feel as though there is a hope in what I am working towards. It can also mean I quit on me. Yielding means complete surrender, stepping aside that the complete process may take place. Understand that when I say "Stepping Aside" I merely mean moving out of my own way. Understand this I have quit on me more times than I care to count. I forfeited a lot of processes. I forfeited because I understood it would require me to be pliable and I was not ready to be. It was going to cause me to be shaped and I was not ready for the commitment. It was not until I came in right relationship with Christ that I was able to fathom that this was only a process and if I surrender it was going to make me better. As I stated in my other book "How *Will You Be Listed?*" "*It* was happening FOR me and not TO me. When we understand this principle, we are then ready to surrender.

So, it was then that I stopped quitting on me, and I surrendered to the will of God. It was not easy. Remember that every ingredient in cake batter serves a purpose. There are some ingredients that you never taste in the actual cake that were placed in the batter. This does not mean they did not serve a purpose. The same is so in being a Servant. You will not always be seen. Some servant roles require you to be in the back. For instance, I write stage plays and I quickly learned to have a healthy respect for the set-up crew. This only came after I had to help with the setup of our first play right after coming off set from being a part of the play and having to set up for the next scene before I go change clothes to be a part of that scene. Talking about TIRED! I was worn out. But at the next play we had people designated specially for set change, this was a major blessing. I no longer had to be in the play and be the play. There are people that need you and they need you to do the work that nobody else desires to do. See we are living in a time where everybody wants credit for what they did. Unfortunately, it does not always happen that way. I considered the set-up crew to also be a part of the cast and once the play was over, I introduced them just like I did the person that carried a lead role. Everybody has a part. Being a Servant requires humility and grace. Everybody does not fit this description. There is nothing wrong with acknowledging the fact that you are not a Servant. The friction comes when one is in denial of their truth yet serving in the role of a Servant. Servants must be created at conception or by process. You do not have to go to school to be a Servant just show up in everyday life and pay attention, this will help teach you to serve. Some serve from a place of need. Some people like being a servant because they need to be doing something, while this is a good thought, this is not a good idea. "If you are not doing it because it is in your heart it will show up through your hands."- Jennifer Johnson Cook. If being a Servant is not in your heart it will show up in the way that you serve. Being a Servant is a beautiful Honor and is not to be taken lightly. Have you ever gone to a wedding reception and helpful Hostesses were in place that made you feel like it was your wedding day? They led you to your seat, pulled out your chair, made sure your glass stayed full and asked if you need anything else after serving you? I am such a sucker for GREAT service. The process, if we surrender to it will also make   us   GREAT   SERVANTS.

SURRENDER TO THE PROCESS, THERE IS A SERVANT WAITING TO BE BIRTHED!!!

Notes

_____

_____

_____

_____

_____

_____

_____

_____

_____

_____

_____

_____

_____

_____

Jennifer Johnson Cook

Do Not Become BITTER in this!

If life has taught me anything it has taught me not to be bitter with the process. The process is designed to work out some things within you. It is formulated specifically for you, though I realize it can frustrate us along the way we cannot afford for it to cause us to become bitter. A bitter lifestyle is a negative lifestyle. God has not created you to be negative nor did He create you to be bitter. I have had several instances in life where I could have walked away and demolish everything that was in my path, but I realized that in doing so I would have accomplished nothing except a torn-up room and probably some sore hands. I realized that being bitter and destructive would only cause things to be hard for me. Please know and fully understand that things have not always been this way. I have had my bitter moments. Yet it was these moments that I learned the lesson that was being taught. I understand that in class to make it to the next class we must first pass the class that we are in. DO NOT STAY THERE!!! There is so much more awaiting you but if you stay in a bitter place you will get bitter results. Life has taught me to wait my turn. As I have said before, so many have gone before me in the very things that I desired of the Lord. I have been left in a hurt, dark place concerning being left behind before but, I got up! I made the choice to get up and live. Too many times I blamed myself for my turn not coming. The truth of the matter is this, whenever it came it was always perfect, I just had to wait my turn. It has also taught me not to judge the situation with my physical eyes but look with my Spiritual eyes to see and accept what God is saying concerning the matter. Things are not always what they appear to be.

Sometimes we must take a deeper look and ask God what we are supposed to see. I know that this may sound super deep but think of it this way, who else is better to ask than the one who made and knows all about you? Right! Nobody but God! I am a firm believer that everything happens for a reason and a purpose and I also believe that there is a lesson to be learned in all things. People often say that I see a lesson in everything. Yes, it is true. Do not get it twisted I am not paranoid I just pay close attention and listen to what God wants me to hear. I feel like if we would pay better attention when things are transpiring in our life, we too will be able to see what is really taking place. You are going to have to see things for what they really are. We often try and camouflage things and as a result we give ourselves a false hope. It is with this type choosing we end up in a make-believe world. This is not good! We end up living a lie. It is a horrible thing to convince yourself that this lie you are living is reality. Life has its fair share of ups and downs but when we see it for what it really is, we can cope with all that it brings. Proverbs 3: 5-6 KJV says it this way- "Trust in the Lord with all thine heart; and lean not unto thine own understanding. 6. In all thy ways acknowledge Him, and He shall direct thy paths." I believe every word of this because I have lived it. The process brings pain but living a lie brings an even greater pain. Many are fearful of the process seeing as how it requires so much at times. A LOT of things I had to surrender to the Lord to go up. If I can do it, I know that you can. It will be worth the surrender, I promise.

_____

_____

_____

_____

_____

_____

_____

_____

_____

_____

_____

_____

_____

_____

Notes

WHAT KEEPS YOU FROM THE PROCESS?

I am going to answer this one. I feel safe sharing my heart with you.

A lot kept me from submitting to the process. My top reason was fear of the unknown. I feared what I had never experienced before, as foolish as this may sound it is the truth for a lot of people. I was afraid that I would be frowned upon. I have had instances in my life where I missed the process because of poor planning. I do believe that if we do not plan properly, we are setting ourselves up for failure. I avoided the process because I knew it would be tedious in a season where I wanted to relax and just be lazy. I did not want to have to focus, pray, fast etc. Understand this,

life has several processes to offer us. I was hesitant about sharing this with you though I desire to offer you hope in the process. So, I am going to share my personal story with you, and it is my prayer that you will get out of my story what is intended for you to receive.......
HERE GOES!

For me, pain and process came early in life. It happened my ninth -grade year of high school. I am going to start by admitting that I did not take school seriously because I wanted to make everybody laugh. I always took pleasure in being the "Class Clown" and I was successful in doing that, but I failed school.

There I was standing at the mailbox reading those red letters that said DETAINED across the top of my report card. I had failed my math class by five points in the ninth grade. "What will I tell my momma?" This was the ONLY question in my head at that time. I could not hide this thing that had taken place if I wanted to go to summer school. Though it was hard, I told her, and she called my siblings and they all chipped in to pay my tuition for summer school. They came through for me as they always did. I love them for the way they love me. However, this time it did not come without a good scolding from them all and my momma. I made them the promise that their money would not be wasted and that I would focus to complete summer school with a passing grade. There I was the first day of summer school with the same teacher in the same classroom doing the same work, with the same unfocused mind! My mind was still focused on foolishness not on work. A recipe for DISASTER! Whenever we enter into anything, we must have a focused mind-set. It is when we fail to do so that we ulti-mately FAIL ourselves and others as well. Yes, I know I made the promise to my sib-lings and my mother that I would get it this time, I know I apologized for not getting it during school. Here I was back to making everybody laugh in summer school. I felt as though it was what I had to do for the day to go well. My teacher pulled me to the side and assured me that I was making a great mistake again and misusing good money. I did better for a few days but that was just so boring. No-body liked math anyway! I persuaded myself that I was only there to make them laugh and enjoy their summer in school. I continued un-til the end with the same momentum. My teacher came back again to let me know that I was in danger of failing his class, I did not take that seriously either. I thought that being in summer school automatically entitled me to a passing grade. Well, I FAILED AGAIN! Yes, the same class, same classroom, same teacher, same work and the same unfocused mind got me the SAME FAILING GRADE once more. There I was in disbelief at the mailbox with yet another RED STAMP of being DETAINED! I thought that this was a bad dream. Well, while all of this failing was going on my uncle died and my mom volunteered me to sing at his funeral. At that time, I was sorely afraid of the deceased. Because I had not told her of my failing yet, I stood beside his coffin and sung like a bird early on a summer morning! That day I realized that there was someone I was more afraid of than the deceased, MY MOMMA! I was afraid that she was going to beat me good for failing my math class again. I sung so well that everyone was paying me sweet compliments after the funeral service had ended. They had no clue I was singing through fear of what my momma was going to do to me. Well, the funeral was over, and a few days had passed, I was on my absolute best behavior. Then there was the question that I dreaded from my mom. "Where is your report card?" I think for a moment or two I fainted while still standing up. I had to tell my mom that hard truth. I whispered these words in the opposite direction "I failed" She exclaimed. "YOU DID WHAT?" I said it again and this time she heard me. I remember my mom being so hurt that I had failed yet another time. At this point I had lost all those cool points that I gained at the funeral. She called my siblings and they expressed their disappointment in me. There was absolutely nothing that I could do about it at this point. After my mom gathered herself, she said "Well you will not get any new school clothes this school year because you are not going to a new grade!" To answer your question, she did not beat me. She said my beating would come daily as I entered the class that I failed twice. She was right. So, I went back to that same classroom with that same teacher but this time I put my desk right beside his facing the chalkboard with my back to a class of ninth graders entering in for the first time... I was determined that I WAS GOING TO GET IT THIS TIME! I studied, I asked questions, I did extra credit work and I even kept his water cup full for him. I was not going to miss it this time. I remained focused because this was not going to happen to me EVER again! When report cards went out at the end of the year it was stamped red again but this time the letters were PRO-MOTED! FINALLY I MADE IT OUT!!!!

That by far WAS one of the most embarrassing times of my life. Yes, I still make people laugh seeing as though I now do comedy but, I know that I can only do so when the time is appropriate. That is why I write stage plays. I have shared this with you that you will know and understand fully that it is possible to make a comeback after a setback. I was proud of myself and I learned something about myself, I COULD FOCUS! Though I could not graduate with my original classmates they never treated me any different and I love them for that. It was 2019 that I finally owned it all. There was a homecoming game in my hometown and each class had a table set up with food so that they could get the opportunity to fellowship. I usually avoided these times because of embarrassment. I finally made the decision to beat fear with fear. I showed up at the homecoming game!

Understand that this is something I was afraid to do each year since graduating from high school in 1996. I would always make an excuse as to why I cannot attend. I not only showed up, I participated with BOTH classes. The class of 1995 (my original graduating class) and the class of 1996 (my graduating class.) Yes, I took pictures with both groups also. That night when I got home I posted BOTH pictures on social media along with the post that said this, "Who gets to rightfully take pictures with two graduating classes? Me!" Funny part is a lot of people didn't recognize I was detained. I did not do this for them, I did it for me. I knew it and it haunted me silently for a long time. Again I say, I did not do this for people, I did it for me. There is something sweet about making up your mind to simply be free. I was not going to rehearse this in my mind another year. I was not going to beat myself up anymore concerning this matter. I was going to be FREE!

Life is just like that, classrooms are everywhere, some classes we must take repeatedly to get the lesson. Sometimes the people that we started with may not be the ones that we finish with and we must know that even this has purpose. I love my classmates from both classes and celebrate with them both. I did not allow my failure to make me bitter towards them. They did what they needed to do to go up so why should I be bitter? NEVER allow your failures to haunt you, HAUNT THEM BACK with acceptance! Do not be ashamed that things did not happen for you the way that they have happened for others . Make it medicine for someone else just like I am doing now.

Such is life. We get left behind in the shuffle and look for everyone else to blame. The biggest issue is that, we do not want to hold ourselves accountable for our own choices. I am here to get you to realize that you must feel the pain, accept the process and enter the sweet promise. Trust that if you must begin again it is totally acceptable. If you must deal with the horrible truth of what really happened and be forced to tell the truth it is perfectly alright. Free yourself to live the life that God has ordained for you to live! Do what you got to do because you are headed somewhere, and you do not have time to see who is keeping score. Truth is if they are keeping your score, they are failing to keep their own. Hold your head up, release that smile. Life is not over, it is just beginning even if it is BEGINNING AGAIN! Though that was bad that happened I would be remised if I did not tell you that I ended up with a teller position at a bank and later promoted to a customer service representative! Yes, the same girl that failed math! I did not allow that to stop me or disqualify myself from applying for the position. I believed that if it were for me nothing would stop me, and nothing did! Not even my past.

You GOT THIS, GO IN GRACE AND RELEASE THAT SMILE AS YOU GO!

_____

_____

_____

_____

_____

_____

_____

_____

_____

_____

_____

_____

_____

STAND

You are going to have to stand on the promises of God! You cannot allow the pain to stop you from entering in. Go in knowing that as the pain gets too great the Lord will share the load. Know that if this is for you, you must journey on. Sometimes the pain is not physical it is mental. It is mentally draining when you find out PROCESS is taking you to uncharted territory. We love being in what is familiar, but we cannot be afraid to venture out if this is what God is leading to. Consider Abram, being told to leave his country, his people and his father's house to go to a land he had never been to before in Genesis 12. That is a type of pain that can be hard to bear, especially when you have gotten acquainted and established where you are. We will find that when it comes to process two of the choices are obey or disobey. If we disobey, we will have to pay and sometimes that price is more that we are able to afford. Whenever we obey even if it hurts or causes us to transition to the uncharted places, we have to know that The Lord Is in fact our Shepherd and He is a Shepherd that takes very good care of His flock! The promise is worth more than your mind can fathom, GO FOR IT! Understand this, sometimes when we stand on what God has led us to do it is not always understood by others. We ought not expect others to understand what God told us. It was told to us because they were our instructions so how will someone else understand? I made some of my biggest mistakes waiting on others to understand what God was leading me to do. Please know there will be instances where confirmation is sent for you through others but do not wait on them to understand what the Lord spoke to you! Stand on what is right, follow the order that is for your steps. Live a life that is pleasing and upright and you will be just fine. I am so excited for you, Greater awaits you!

_____

_____

_____

_____

_____

_____

_____

_____

_____

_____

_____

_____

_____

The Pain, The Process, The Promise

_____

_____

_____

_____

_____

_____

_____

_____

_____

_____

_____

_____

_____

_____

Conclusion

GO IN PEACE, YOU HAVE WORK TO DO!

Trust the Process though it will involve pain of some sort. The promise that will be released after this will cause you to forget the pain that was caused, the same is so in giving birth! PRESS ON! BIRTH IT! THE WORLD AWAITS YOU NOW!

A look at THE AUTHOR:

Evangelist Jennifer Johnson Cook

is the daughter of Mr. Isaac and the late "Mrs. Ruby W. Johnson both formerly of Bishopville SC. Jennifer was born and raised in Bishopville, SC. She is a 1996 Alumni of Bishopville High School as well as a 2011Alumni of Kenneth Shuler School of Cosmetology, Columbia SC as a Licensed Cosmetologist and a 2012 graduate of this school as a Licensed Cosmetology Instructor. Jennifer is DELIGHTFULLY married to Mr. Rodney R. Cook and with God's help they parent three loving, gifted children, Rodneya, Janiyah and Jeremiah

Jennifer accepted her call into ministry in 2003 and has been fulfilling "THE CALL" ever since! Jennifer and her husband are humbled to partner in ministry by way of Stage plays and short skits with God's grace and guidance, the most recent one was, "Come to the Light" May 2017. She has also starred in a movie addressing domestic violence and child abuse entitled, "Escaped to Tell." In 2020 she yielded to the assignment of being an Author.

Be it through the Word of song, Evangelizing, Prayer, Stage plays, skits, styling hair, or by the words of a book, Jennifer firmly believes that the word of God is not to be confined by the four walls of the Local Church. She believes that the WORLD is her parish, and with the help of God she will spread the Word to all mankind!

Jennifer Johnson Cook

Pure Thoughts Publishing, LLC